CW00474192

PERSIAN MINIATURES

Mimi Khalvati

A BELFAST KISS

David Morley

Smith/Doorstop Books

British Library Cataloguing in Publication Data
Khalvati, Mimi, *1944* -
    Persian miniatures.
    1. Poetry in English, 1945. Anthologies
    I. Title II. Morley, David, *1964* — . Belfast kiss
    821.91408

ISBN 1 869961 25 0

Published by Smith/Doorstop Books
The Poetry Business
51 Byram Arcade
Westgate
Huddersfield HD1 1ND

Cover design by Francis Noon
Typeset at The Poetry Business

Acknowledgements:

Mimi Khalvati: *The North, Writing Women, Poetry Durham, PN Review, Poetry Review*

David Morley:BBC Radio Cumbria, BBC World Service, *London Magazine, The Echo Room, The North, The Rialto, Stand Magazine, Northern Poetry Vol 1* (Littlewood Press 1989), *Poetry Introduction 7* (Faber & Faber 1990), *New Lakes Poets* (Bloodaxe Books 1990) Thanks are also due to the Tyrone Guthrie Centre, Irish Republic, where most of the 'Belfast' poems were written.

CONTENTS

Mimi Khalvati

David Morley

PERSIAN MINIATURES

Mimi Khalvati

EVERGREEN

It was past green fields and pines
the Jews were cattled and the last thing
her witch's eyes could see – thirteen
million pairs they say – was the green
of the hill turning away like a mother
turning to take her children home.

And I have lived with green in playing-fields,
neighbours' gardens seeping poison
through the fence: ground-elder flaunting
height and health where colour should have been,
the colours of my childhood, needed more than ever
in a land that has adopted me, that turns me grey;

while the dress my mother danced in, yellow
sun-spots in the flounces, circles on its own,
sad as olde-time vaudeville, and camel, camel-
lilac of the slopes where shepherds' lives
meet poppy every day, has settled on the leaves
of war and every leaf has turned.

Even blues are not the same: of tiles,
of domes, of skies too dazed for blue;
or of shadows, mulberry-blue, in the room
you enter blinded, learning how to see again
gloom becoming someone dear, a grandmother
who gives you grapes she has quietly washed.

And white, like all the colours of the world
raising home, hazy as the verandahs
you half-remember, is something to avoid
in a land where no one's hands are clean;
where dust is never sand but more a mirage
no one even yearns for, intent on lawns.

A PERSIAN MINIATURE

(Shirin committing suicide over Khusraw's coffin)

She said: take a picture, an art postcard –
I took this Persian miniature – then take
the top right-hand corner and describe it ...

Well ... it looks like a face; two of the arches
that march across the background look like eyebrows –
not Persian eyebrows meeting in the middle –
but intersected by a nose, a pillar.
The nose has peeled and left a patch that looks
rather like a map of The British Isles.

The top left-hand corner she said to use
for the second verse – here I am on cue –
is also a face, only this one's nose,
believe it or not, sports a large pink map
of America, or at least, the West Coast.
As if to banish doubts, a sea of stars
beneath it waves the flag. You see how hard
it is, how far away one gets from art,
and sixteenth century Persian art at that.

Well, the third and final stanza – although
I can't imagine how I'll ever get it
all in one – is to take the two inch square
at the bottom centre of the picture,
describe it, wrap it up and there you are,
you've got your poem. O.K. Three lines left:
Shirin and Khusraw (Romeo and Juliet)
are dying; he's in agony; she,
though spraying blood on him, seems quite at peace.

So. That's hardly the place to end a poem.
It's interesting, though, to think: here is England
on the right, America on the left
and caught between the two, like earth itself
twin-cornered by the eyes of gods, Iran's
most famous lovers lie, watched and dying.
How could a painter in Shiraz have known,
four hundred years ago, of this? Has time
rewritten him? Or was it always so?

Has power always called for sacrifice,
the dream of love on earth to trade itself
for paradise, the 'Rose that never blows
so red as where some buried Caesar bled?'
And still the fountain flows from bowl to bowl,
from lips of stone to fields, from mines to graves;
and there, in Zahra's Paradise for Martyrs,
still bears the 'Hyacinth the Garden wears
Dropt in her Lap from some once lovely Head.'

Zahra's Paradise: the war cemetery in Tehran

SEVENSES

At seven, skirting a verandah, pausing to seduce
an arabesque from heaven down to a pirouette, I entrance
the lovers from their leaning shapes under the shade
of scaffolding to applaud for encores whose echoes on an island
describe my cause in cups inscribed with my difficult
name. I dance to its tune, newly pronounced.

At forty-two, meeting a man who's close on forty-nine,
turning the land on a dig to find slivers of time
to patch the potter's clay, I treasure what is found,
what is mine, glance at the vessels on the ground, my ware;
failing to define the chalice in the air, I resign myself
to the figures' stoop in rings within rings of the dance.

THE WAITING HOUSE

> *'Tem Eyos Ki went to the waiting house to pass her sacred time in a sacred place, sitting on moss and giving her inner blood to the Earth Mother ... she smiled, and sang ... of a place so wondrous the minds of people could not even begin to imagine it ... But sometimes a woman will think she hears a song, or thinks she remembers beautiful words, and she will weep a little for the beauty she almost knew. Sometimes she will dream of a place that is not like this one.'* Anne Cameron, *Daughters of Copper Woman*

And I will bring you sweetmeats of stars
     and four leaf clover
and plait your hair in grassknot braid
     that maidens weave
on holy days when streets are strewn
     with widows' weeds;
and I will rub your spine with persian essence
     rose and lime
and stroke the down that tingling purrs of home.

And you will sing me songs my mother
     used to sing
of pomegranates' stubborn juice sluiced
     off silver trays
and rounded limbs in old hammams; and tales
     of Taghi
at the kitchen-gate, gaunt and thin, slung
     like a tinker's mule
with children's billycans, the smell of onion
     taunting him.

And you will numb my rootless moan in murmurings,
                    bird of my breastbone
quieten, its sobbing still, its flailing wings;
                    and we will sit
in the waiting house, latticed by the sea,
                    in purdah drawn
by our sheet of hair, your cheek-bone's arc
                    half-lit;
and we will croon and whisper till the hardening
                    yellow dawn

strikes on the mud where crabs peer out to pan
                    like periscopes;
then laying down on curling moss our ghosting
                    shadows' twine
in sieve of nature's palm, you will give me
                    your dreams
and I will give you mine and dreaming still
                    your blood
will live, as mine in yours, in mine.

RICE

I
Ten years later, I recognise his profile in a Tehran cab.
You see these teeth, he said, leaning across the passengers,
what became of me? ... I see him silhouetted in dazzle
as the tunnel ends on the last lap to Frankfurt, his hand
on the window's metal lip, his cap in the other circling
like a bird – then, loosed on the wind, beating a tattoo

against the wires as I watch him reach to the rack for his case,
send that too struggling through the window, socks and all.
I have come, he declared, *to start at the start ...* Now, a decade
later, he asks: *You see these teeth?* He bares them in the light
to show how short, how straight they are. *What became of me:*
you wonder why? His fist emerges from his pocket, clenched.

I eat it all the time. My hand is never still, like a swallow
at its nest, going in, going out. Not a grain escapes.
He fingers his moustache. *I even check in wing-mirrors.*
See how it's worn my teeth right down? His hand unfurls,
dabs at the proffered air between us. *Please, have some.*
What, raw? I ask. *It's rice,* he urges. *Rice.*

II
I have fled on mules, the star of Turkey in my sky, to start
at the start. I have come like sleet with Mary in the dark; swum
into hedgerows by the line. Gifts of weave and leather tucked
in polythene for friends, already fled or free, are dry.
Will they harbour us, we wonder, ten years, a revolution later,
towel us from swollen rivers chanting *MARG BAR EMRIKA* * ?

III
The cabs still carry passengers; my mother in her black chador,
my sisters among soldiers, now and then a face blasted
like a cake. They have granted me asylum. I write plays.
A friend I love in London has hung the kurdish mules
I brought her on the same hook as an old sitar she never
plays. When she dusts them she thinks of me, and of rivers.

I told her of the man I met twice: once in a train,
once again in Tehran in those early days ... what days they were ...
Ah well. Her sister lives near Washington; the husband – an Iranian –
works for the Department of Defence, and for real estate; comes home
to scan The Post, its leaders on Japan: po-faced as she snatches
victory from jaws set ever closer as they wing towards Potomac.

*Death to America

WARTIME PICNIC

On the verandah
the wet-nurse thinks of her own
pomegranate-tree.

The river paddles
as we barbecue; Hassan
removes his serge-green.

I climb the noon-day
peak: a broken flip-flop thong
flutters at my feet.

CHILDREN OF HIROSHIMA

On a good-girl Sunday afternoon
walking with my mother in Regent's Park
linking arms like signoras and signorinas
in piazzas we have visited, we talk a language
of our own, happy to be overheard, free
to be personal in level voices mingling
Farsi with Latin and the smell of roses.

A royal occasion, she a slip of a girl
honoured by an invitation to be one of the maidens
who bring in trays for the bride, heaped
with petals from the rainbow on the peacock lawn,
their names as strange as Woburn Abbey,
Centifolia Bullata and Paddy McGredy –
is a story I have already half-forgotten.

I see the yellow roses where we stood.
Each bed was perfect. Each favourite superseded
until our backs began to ache and we headed
for the car, our separate lives forking
like the path by the gate, leaving stoic
heathers and old-age pensioners together
to mind the cold, colder in the grate.

One bed alone was trampled. Near the gate.
Just as we were leaving. Just one bed.
As though a heavy weight had come down on it,
from nowhere. Long-stemmed pink roses
clustered in rings like bridesmaids' wreaths
were pressing to the ground as though a boot,
a giant boot, was holding down their heads;

as though they alone had been singled out
to bear the brunt of hurricanes, some mean
revenge, some poison rising from the soil
to sap the strength their neighbours had,
so pristine in their regiments, to resist
whatever scourge laid low this bed.
From above or below? I looked for signs.

There was only one: CHILDREN OF HIROSHIMA.
Children of Hiroshima? It doesn't make sense.
So some breeder allows his conscience to play
name-games with small pink roses ...
but what has happened to the bed? Why this bed?
When my children are sick I hide it from my mother.
But now I need her eyes, her wonder. I show her.

Children of Hiroshima. She pronounces it differently.
She is shocked. My shock seems greater than hers.
I whip her up. She is moved to tears. Are they real?
I protect the roses. I wish I hadn't told her.
She keeps on talking. I keep on talking.
We exchange analyses; handicapped by horticultural
foolishness, and Farsi. We turn to English.

Patting herself, her hand ungloved, as though someone
had stolen her wealth, my mother says:
I shall never forget this as long as I live.
And I feel like the child she kept on telling:
I live only for you, if it weren't for you,
my darling ... as sceptical, as guilty, as lonely
as the child who vowed to live only for herself.

A THANK YOU LETTER

How lucid every arc, every plane, every mote
on lacquer's ebony. The ivory keys
are quiet. There is no music. Space
reflects me in its symmetry. A light.
A wall. A shadow. And I alone in it.

Here a cushion. There a rug. A picture
hangs, the name of she who gave it,
the names of all these people, he who
chose it, she who wove it for all these
facets I have lived, earning the gift.

Here is Mahmoud dead and gone, Simin
lost in the backrooms of Tehran and what
happened to the girl who wove kelims?
She named her daughter after me, sowing me
in someone I may never see: Maryam.

How loved I have been. Come and see
my room. The stems beneath the surfaces
are light as old calligraphy. But the beauty
you will feel is in the care with which I laundered,
smoothed, placed in perfect harmony

the names of those who loved me: like portraits
in a shrine of all who have died in a family.
As I near the alcove someone has reserved
for me in the iconography of memory for my
children to turn to from the growing horrors

of their day, I am grateful for the gentleness
of losing flesh-and-bloodness in gifts
I will leave like gravestones or, less grave,
in the airs that will age into elegies if I choose
to play some music, to remain oblivious. P.S.

I remember now the name of the girl
who wove kelims: Mundegar –
it means *she who remains.*

TURNING THE PAGE

This grey
is made more bearable
by the thought of sun
on your own brown skin
just over the horizon

and this loneliness
looking over its shoulder
at its own old absence
looks forward too
to a merry death

and the lucky West Indian
in a language that can be,
when all's said, at least read
by oppressors, hopes
to honour his grandmother:

but what if every time
the thought was struck dead
as the tree where you kissed
in the mule-shade
of a glade in Damavand*?

What if the city
that gave credence to your sickness
were as vanished as the home
you took for granted you would bless
with success and happy children:

were now as alien as the dun
of another tongue, of freckled skin?
Would you turn to the dying —
take a leaf from their book? —
To history, Russia for example?

How dead would a page be
without the smile you drew
(in brackets) on the face
of a sun, of a country
on the other side?

> *Damavand mountain, north of Tehran, that gives its name
> to an area of the town in its foothills*

STONE OF PATIENCE

'In the old days', she explained to a grandchild bred in England,
'in the old days in Persia, it was the custom to have a stone,
a special stone you would choose from a rosebed, or a goat-patch,
a stone of your own to talk to, tell your troubles to,
a stone we called as they now call me, *sang-é-saba.'*

No therapists then to field a question with another,
but stones from dust where ladies' fingers, cucumbers
basked in sun. Were the ones they used for gherkins
babies that would have grown, like piano tunes had we known
the bass beyond the first few bars? Or miniatures?

Some things I'm content to guess: colour in a calyx-tip,
is it gold or mauve? A girl or a boy ... Patience
was so simple then: waiting for the clematis to open,
to purple on a wall; the bud to shoot out stamens,
the jet of milk to leave its rim like honey

on the bee's fur. But patience when the cave is sealed,
a boulder at the door, is riled by the scent of hyacinth
in the blue behind the stone: the willow by the pool
where once she sat to trim a beard with kitchen scissors,
to tilt her hat at smiles, at sleep, at congratulations.

And a woman, faced with a lover grabbing for his shoes
when women friends would have put themselves in hers,
no longer knows what's virtuous. Will anger shift
the boulder, buy her freedom, and the earth's? Or patience,
like the earth's, be abused? Even nonchalance

can lead to courage, to conception: a voice that says
oh come on darling, it'll be alright, oh do let's.
How many children were born from words such as these?
I know my own were; now learning to repeat them, to outgrow
a mother's awe of consequences her body bears.

So now that midsummer, changing shape, has brought in
another season, the grape becoming raisin, hinting
in a nip at the sweetness of a clutch, one fast upon another;
now that the breeze is raising sighs from sheets
as she tries to learn again, this time for herself,

to fling caution to the winds like colour in a woman's skirt
or to borrow patience from the stones in her own backyard
where fruit still hangs on someone else's branch ... don't ask her
whose? as if it mattered. Say: *they won't mind*
as you reach for a leaf, for the branch, and pull it down.

'THE POPPY SIGNALS TIME TO SCYTHE THE WHEAT'

I quote my mother though I don't suppose
she scanned it quite like that but found a brief
and simpler way to say that poppy grows
when wheat is ripe, like anger, love or grief.
For anger cannot foster change when dumb
to fault a man, nor love that cannot scythe
his pride fulfil him; grief will not succumb
to guilt that bears a grudge to bear a wreath.
No anger, love or grief will harvest good
till men can learn to listen, women learn
to speak, and turn their dreams to likelihood
of change and peace, redress and union.
　　　　The day he died my mother cried all night,
　　　　her tendrils round me, wound towards the light.

EARL'S COURT

I brush my teeth harder when the gum bleeds.
Arrive alone at parties, leaving early.

The tide comes in, dragging my stare
from pastures I could call my own.

Through the scratches on the record – *Ah! Vieni, vieni!* –
I concentrate on loving.

I use my key. No duplicate of this.
Arrive alone at parties, leaving early.

I brush my teeth harder when the gum bleeds.
Sing to the fern in the steam. Not even looking:

commuters buying oranges, Italian vegetables,
bucket flowers from shores I might have danced in, briefly.

I use my key: a lost belonging on the stair.
Sing to the fern in the steam. I wash my hair.

The tide goes out, goes out. The body's wear and tear.
Commuters' faces turn towards me: bucket flowers.

A man sits eyeing destinations on the train.
He wears Islamic stubble, expensive clothes, two rings.

He talks to himself in Farsi, loudly like a drunk.
Laughs aloud to think where life has brought him.

Eyeing destinations on the train – a lost belonging –
talks to himself with a laugh I could call my own.

Like a drunk I want to neighbour him; sit beside
his stubble's scratch: turn his talking into chatting.

I want to tell him I have a ring like his,
only smaller. I want to see him use his key.

I want to hear the child who runs to him call
Baba! I want to hear him answer, turning

from his hanging coat: *Beeya, Babajune, beeya!*
Ah, Vieni. vieni! ...

*from the duet of Madame Butterfly and Pinkerton

RUBAIYAT

for Telajune

Beyond the view of crossroads ringed with breath
her bed appears, the old-rose covers death
has smoothed and stilled; her fingers lie inert,
her nail-file lies beside her in its sheath.

The morning's work over, her final chore
was 'breaking up the sugar' just before
siesta, sitting cross-legged on the carpet,
her slippers lying neatly by the door.

The image of her room behind the pane,
though lost as the winding road shifts its plane,
returns on every straight, like signatures
we trace on glass, forget and find again.

I have inherited her tools: her anvil,
her axe, her old scrolled mat, but not her skill;
and who would choose to chip at sugar blocks
when sugar-cubes are boxed beside the till?

The scent of lilacs from the road reminds me
of my own garden: a neighbouring tree
grows near the fence. At night its clusters loom
like lantern-moons, pearly-white, unearthly.

I don't mind that the lilac's roots aren't mine.
Its boughs are, and its blooms. It curves its spine
towards my soil and litters it with dying
stars: deadheads I gather up like jasmine.

My grandmother would rise and take my arm,
then sifting through the petals in her palm
would place in mine the whitest of them all:
"Salaam, dokhtaré-mahé-man, salaam!"

'Salaam, my daughter-lovely-as-the-moon!'
Would that the world could see me, Telajune,
through your eyes! Or that I could see a world
that takes such care to tend what fades so soon.

A BELFAST KISS

KISS

David Morley

'Some streets listed in this section are no longer in existence. By still listing non-existent streets we therefore give the user of this guide a close location to future developments.'
Belfast Street Directory

A BELFAST KISS

> *Once a man was discovered by his wife she'd wait until he was*
> *sleeping, then give him the Belfast kiss: a broken bottle around his*
> *face* – Intelligence Officer, 1 Para

> *The Passenger got out, grabbed the Armalite, and was gunned down*
> *by the lads; he survived ... the lads sustained him with the kiss of life*
> – Corporal, King's Own Royal Border

I. Silences

Somewhere, on a housing list, biro skid-marks
over a name; somewhere, the bruise, where chalk
smashed against a defiant, opened desk-lid;
somewhere, a statistic, dovetailing into small talk;
somewhere, a nurse changes a burnt girl's tampax ...
These are things which words are finished with:
the checkpoint, the soldier's story: *We got to the barracks –*
there was this little tot, identical to my niece.
She never said a word, just started to walk
towards me, then spat in my face.

II. Orangemen

The barmen all have featherweight ulcers
jabbing their bellies. Butterflies for the rest.
Grant them wings to outfly their past,
orange-veined migrations down the histories of Ulster.
Stories reach me in the bar, overheard
and noted till they start giving me the eye.
Then, one of Paisley's disciples questions me,
and my answer's in an accent they've heard
backing agreements ... Until a UVF, gone in the head
on *Bushmills*, starts shoring me up: *Words*

are fucking powerful, and we always had
that edge on the Taigs. So, they talk at once,
calling me *my friend,* putting to me the crunch
question: *And what do you reckon to Hillsborough?*
That words are fucking powerful, though
who forms those sentences, owns the teeth and tongue,
is the crunch answer. And I remember the graffitist:
SIX TAIGS DON'T FIT IN A THREE MAN GRAVE. RAMBO STONE.
MILLTOWN CEMETERY. MARCH '88. HA-HA. God,
grant them words, covenants. You were the last artist.

III. Reprisal

He had a job, was on the long uphill
from dole, testing the composure of brick walls
in the burned-out terraces of Shankill.
Starlings refurbished their former shit-holes.
The pigeons were already in place, like slates.
Graffiti was washed from the peace line that evening:
red/white/blue/green blood sopped from a guillotine.
When he knocked through a wall, saw the crates
of petrol lined up for milking, when he
legged up the road for the RUC,

he had a job, was on the long uphill from dole;
he was testing the composure of brick walls.
Pigeons and starlings bickered like motives,
flattering his eye with nondescript colour.
He had a job, was on the long uphill,
when neighbours came round, took him to the Falls,
and left him, bellowing, in his own torn semen
in the muck of a safe house, scratched from a cellar.
He was in a dark river, testing the composure of salmon,
when a hook twitched him sideways. He had to dive.

IV. Squaddie

On the ring-road, a ferrocrete dolmen
of flyovers. I came up an underpass
like I was breaking surface
under a sky that takes seconds to cave in.
Then: the cardboard cut-out of Divis Flats.
Those jigsawn counties – Leitrim, Cavan –
have a missed corner here. Journey and arrival
grows obtuse, pathetic *(walks up towards me, then spat*
in my face). I'm thought a big man –
look up, never down: that's survival,

pure nous, the sort as wins trophies
back in barracks: *I got posted here*
on instructions as logical
as Belfast. Shankill, Ballymurphy –
I can take them, no hassle.
In the evenings we pull boxer
shorts on, punch merry fuck out of each other.
Regimental spirit. And the air needs cleared.
No worse than Toxteth. Kids in good schools.
You get into routine if it fucking kills.

V. Disposal

'The job was to blow open the boot, but the car
had sagged on its axles, looking for all the world
like the body was in the back, and the tyres fired
to detonate evidence'. *Come and tell me if it's your father.*
'Then: the short of it: the body had been wired.
So we got a hook and gave a pull. He didn't
fall to pieces, but left most of his head'.
Is it him? 'But they'd got word,
blew the pavement while we curled
with the first blast'. *Yes. No. It isn't.*

VI. Cross-Border

Old paddy from the old days of the nail bomb;
proddy from his petrol and brick: both bang
up to date. The last leaves cartwheel into flame
with the *rapprochment* of winter. A Land Rover
edges up the faint tracks of a Mourne mountain.
Invisible. Within one acre of terrain
three men trawl a peat-bed for cover,
squinny through gunsights, whisper of a cross: claim
and counter-claim. What they stammer they sing
through hand-radios; ghost-clatter of Somme,

Mt. Tumbledown. Below them: a shed, obsolete ark
marooned on a moorside. A curlew flutes its soap-bubble
– a glistening memory breaking on their faces.
So they rush the outhouse, tug out these tubes
of explosive packed tight as Durex –
sausage-meat Semtex. On Carlingford Lough,
a patrol picks up their suspect. Under duress
(Doc Marten in the bollocks, lighter flicked on pubes),
he confesses: to visiting his niece,
to going out of his way (moorland, Mourne) to avoid trouble.

VII. Provisional

I have lived in importunate places, grenades
soft on my palm as spuds. The back-yards,
where I grew, boasted the only orchard
east-side of Derry. Apples and pears,
windfall of battered autumnals,
sagged on my mother's apron as she cropped
the reds and greens. I would salt the water
where they hung cleaning and rubbing: bobbed
under from my gobbling Hallowe'en teeth, salt
prickling my tongue as I scrunched their sides.

When the storm blew up in '69,
ours was the first harvest. They'd time
recruitment to our age at CSE,
then fetch us in our greenery.
A mural spattered the terrace-end with primary
colours; a barricade sprouted strawberry fire;
a petrol bomb ballooned my father's tree;
they came to take us ... Now, I wire
traps in worm-holes, snares in fruit,
grass whispering my name and date.

VIII. Kiss

In the mechanism of a child's throat:
a template of staves, octaves, baby-talk
bubbles, poetries of attention-seeking ...
The hurting side is gone, but in my mind
Heather is still there, a baby.
The sawn edge of a shotgun, seething
through a caravan's ersatz coat —
rabid, percussive ... *When you find*
your child like that, quiet, as though she
had dreamed through it all, you want to walk

up to the fuckers who did it and burn them, slowly.
Sunlight topples the last galleries of Divis;
a bus grinds fuel on the grass of Falls.
(He will burn them slowly, atom by atom).
I knelt to kiss her, then I saw the flex
trailing from her wrist to her legs ...
A mirror of sheet-iron crashes
from the roof of Unity Flats. (He
wanted to kiss her, atom by atom;
atom by atom, to dream through it all) ...

ARMAGH PATROL

I await developments with the cast of mind
of a pike-angler: repeated throws around
this country; nothing dragged at my reel but weed,
or the tension of attention ... But the road
spooling through Lisburn had its moments
and its teeth. I was hurdling the fence
of my barracks to a Land Rover, hunched there
on a bypass, when I caught the bomb-flash of a flare,
then another, and another, till my whole eye was netted ...

Gone to seed now, I lie, listening on my bed
to whatever swims from the radio to my ear:
Home News, shipping forecast – *Rockall, Finisterre* -
casting about me, head snarled in iced flannel
– God, toss back this blindness –
                              Dogger, Fair Isle ...

SAFE HOUSE

She doesn't know it, but he will have the lot
– bed, breakfast, and the last hot water.
The grain of the bed-board will grunt at leisure;
a moth, swivelling on a window, will face about.

Even now, she's mawkish over his question,
how 'a night spent alone is spent*forever?*'
Cue the 'cut suit', bottle, the Falls lingua franca ...
Yes, she'll take a gin. Go easy on the lemon.

(Morning, he approves her nipples, *Ready Brek,* coil ...).
The clock's ticking by his ear is more than relevant;
ditto his fast motorbike in its esurient oil;
ditto the Armalite from the last tenement.

She says, *Shite like as you open my door,*
then, *Get from here, love, or stay forever.*

KEEPING ST. PATRICK'S

A car-park balloons from the bus depot
in a womb of wheels. Belfast's *nouveau riche*
tramp by in a mural of departing saints.
They are ferrying via Larne to stake a heart
in a forest of vampires. By Stranraer, by Glasgow,
along an unmoved nerve of British Rail,
they go hunting a caress, a bitter stout.

Then, sunlight throws them off: through a cloud
of exhaust and steam, a squall of hail
fists the windscreens. They cannot go
without watching the light tilt its skirts
at this dead-pan estuary. Remembering the date
and duty-free, they line niches
of the passenger-lounge, keeping to the shadows.

JERUSALEM

Ballymurphy painted white, inside and out;
road-blocked suburbs, then the accomplishment
of a bounding wall to stop the desert's
abstract itch. This achieved, we grew fluent

in our dialogues: the limit on sense
was vox pop, as was ambivalence
about a noun for boredom. Came the day
a master of lexicography

motorbike-jumped the lower wall-sectors
and made off for the border. He was taken alive,
displayed in the central archives
(after public vasectomy and grammar –

confiscation), writing, rewriting
in blackened sand, *Lift up your hearts and sing.*

PAISLEYITES

We were castaways, outlanders,
beyond any pale of thrown cold water,
piling dynamite from Sunday tea,
out of our crammed electricity.
Until, gradually, we grew no less
the enemy than a mirror braced
against a wall, or a pond, looked-into
with its bike tyre and rush-hour minnows;
shadows gurning through a mask, the faces
of policemen alleging truancy, vandalism.
We hate. It freezes on the lash of an eye,
rimes the husk of every answer we promise.
We lob the half-brick that slams through this vision.
Now are we mighty. Hear the phlegm in our cry.

SENTRY HILL: A STORY

The brother died young, at home;
the child in the yellow photograph,

restored and sneering in your room.
Too often you would talk about his music

– the fugues mouldering,
locked in a suitcase under his bed –

and decided that some other misunderstood
genius was rewriting them this very moment.

If any of this were actually true.

I love him without knowing him.
No-one remembered him but you.

I don't ask any questions; now
there is no point, now I am alone to know

of his existence: washed-up
on the dreg of a small Ulster farm.

And yet you will say, as Montale
once whispered, *how easy it is*

to love a shadow, myself always
trying to be shadow

if any of this were true.

THE POLITICISATION OF THE NORTH WIND

We came out safe, under the aspens; wanted
the road south, but winds deflected
our point of reference to the motorway.
A Police Rover winks on its orbit round
an arterial lane. Cobs of leaf-litter give way
to a blackbird's enquiry. Ivy dripfeeds
an oak, as if accidentally. We need
the road south, but accidents are happening.
A rescue party sifts the rubble of falling
leaves; a hand of the law harries us down turn-offs
— its flickered blue flame; a kestrel makes its one-off
bid in a plunging market. We circle a bend
with a sign saying *Motorway Regulations Terminate Here.*
Aspens. Wind. Regulations terminate here.

ENNISKILLEN

There was a speedboat ploughing up Lough Erne,
an activity I thought the local RUC
would take no shine to.
I watched three little grebes make with the rhythm.

Imagine my discomfiture when the boatman waved
then a four-eyed warden told me to push off.
I plucked up my fag-ends, enough, never enough;
followed lager cans to the centre of Enniskillen,

a place, now, infamous as Walsingham, and shrine
to all discomfiture. I felt a lot for a heaven
whose latest queue
still wore their Remembrance poppies
as though they'd just left the nave
where the priest held back, half-listening for — rain.

JACKDAW BLUES

I select my best shotgun – a Berren .22.
I'm a Monaghan farmer. I've got work to do.

Jackdaws are prickling the edge of my mind.
I'm tired of vermin and I'm tired of time.

The crops rise up like sentries there.
You can't whistle money out of thin air.

These birdies are shillings to throw away.
I can take their begging, but I take my pay.

Over the border, the prices are low.
Those beaks in my wallet have to go.

I'd a son shot by terrorists over the way.
Like, he was begging. They blew him away.

Sometimes I wonder if they feel the shot
before the gun-crack scatters the lot.

I'm begging too – a gun is my prayer.
I can make dust like God. Yes, out of thin air.

Them jackdaws squat black: dead fruit on my trees.
I remember the priest: his gaggle of fees.

I remember the missus... she moved as she died
towards the priest's hand. He shrugged and sighed.

One death such as this won't add to the others,
he murmured. He'd forgotten my brother's.

The gun on my arm won't steady if I cry.
The gun in my heart's self-loaded till I die.

SHELLEY IN IRELAND

You can see why he did it: Coleridge
    in London; Wordsworth
   hedgehogging through winter at Grasmere;
    Southey snapping the cards down – ... *God!* ... *God!*
And in the *Keswick Cumberland Pacquet*
of 28 January 1812:

... Mr. Shelley alarmed by an
    unusual noise,
   was knocked down by ruffians, and had
    remained senseless for a time. Being
at Chestnut Cottage (Keswick), a seat of
Gideon Dare (Esq). And Mr. Dare was

not best pleased. Sailing from Whitehaven
    (assassination
   meant England), they gate-crashed Ireland
in Dublin, he took stock of his pistles,
dashed off 'Address to the Irish people';

(content in short: *downright proposals –*
    the society
   of peace and love). You can see where he
   was aiming: those severed, sacred words:
liberté, fraternité ... And the rest? –
baskets below his guillotining trust.

That he never picked up a printer's
    tab's not pertinent –
   knowing a shared slab of poverty
   would some day pay off with the jack-pot
– quids of visionary blood on the streets ...
Romanticism. *There* was the cheque you

slapped your name on, finding it'd bounce
    like Byron's bollocks
  on the thighs of that importuned Age.
    Zeitgeist willing, but the flesh went weak –
Ireland quit Shelley. A weeping headwind
rinsed out the mist from the storm of his eye.

Mimi Khalvati and David Morley are the joint winners in The Poetry Business Poetry Competition 1989.

MIMI KHALVATI was born in Tehran in 1944, but came to England at the age of six. She trained as an actress and worked in rep and film before going back to Iran to run a theatre group. Since her return to England in 1973 she has directed plays on the fringe, toured Israel with her one-woman show, designed and produced dolls houses and puppet theatres, and published a children's book. She lives in North London with her son and daughter.

Her work is appearing in Anvil's *New Voices 1990*. She was co-winner of the Afro-Caribbean Prize in the Peterloo Poets Open Poetry Competition 1990.

DAVID MORLEY is of Romany descent. He was born in Blackpool in 1964. He read Zoology at Bristol University, and has completed research on the effect of acid rain in Cumbria. He is founder and director of Poetry Network, an international organisation for integrating approaches to science and the arts, and he runs workshops and writing placements in educational establishments throughout the North of England.

He won a Tyrone Guthrie Award in 1988 and a major Gregory Award in 1989. He was a major prizewinner in the Index on Censorship Poetry Competition 1989 and the Northern Poetry Competition 1989. His first collection *Releasing Stone* was published by Nanholme Press in 1989.

For details of the current Competition, our Reading Service, The North Magazine, and details of books in print, write to: The Poetry Business, Floor 4, The Byram Arcade, Westgate, Huddersfield HD1 1ND, enclosing a stamped addressed envelope.